EX LIBRIS

Speak, Old Parrot

Dannie Abse

HUTCHINSON
LONDON

Published by Hutchinson 2013

1 3 5 7 9 10 8 6 4 2

First published in Great Britain in 2013 by
Hutchinson
Random House, 20 Vauxhall Bridge Road,
London SW1V 2SA

www.randomhouse.co.uk

Addresses for companies within The Random House Group Limited can
be found at: www.randomhouse.co.uk/offices.htm

The Random House Group Limited Reg. No. 954009

A CIP catalogue record for this book is available
from the British Library

ISBN 9780091944643

The Random House Group Limited supports The Forest Stewardship
Council® (FSC®), the leading international forest-certification organisation.
Our books carrying the FSC label are printed on FSC®-certified paper.
FSC is the only forest-certification scheme supported by the leading
environmental organisations, including Greenpeace. Our paper
procurement policy can be found at
www.randomhouse.co.uk/environment

Typeset in Bembo by Palimpsest Book Production Limited,
Falkirk, Stirlingshire
Printed and bound in Great Britain by Clays Ltd, St Ives plc

Dante once prepared to paint an angel.
Whom to please? You whisper 'Beatrice'.

Robert Browning

Contents

Acknowledgements

Some of these new poems appeared in *In Extra Time*, an Enitharmon limited edition. Others were first published in *Acumen*, the *Guardian*, *Homage to Eros* (Robson), *Answering Back* (Picador), *London Magazine*, *Modern Poetry in Translation*, *New Statesman*, *Poetry London*, *PN Review*, *Poetry Review* and *Poetry Wales*.

'Portrait of an Old Doctor' is an earlier poem revised, and 'Song of the Crow' is after Primo Levi. 'Rilke's Confession' originated from several lines of his I encountered many years ago.

I thank Siân Williams for her help in the preparation of the manuscript of this book and for her perdurable engagement with my work which matches that of my long-time editor at Hutchinson, Anthony Whittome.

Talking to Myself

In the mildew of age
all pavements slope uphill

slow slow
towards an exit.

It's late and light allows
the darkest shadow to be born of it.

Courage, the ventriloquist bird cries
(a little god, he is, censor of language)

remember plain Hardy and dandy Yeats
in their inspired wise pre-dotage.

I, old man, in my new timidity,
think how, profligate, I wasted time

– those yawning postponements on rainy days,
those paperhat hours of benign frivolity.

Now Time wastes me and there's hardly time
to fuss for more vascular speech.

The aspen tree trembles as I do
and there are feathers in the wind.

Quick quick
speak, old parrot,
do I not feed you with my life?

The Old Gods

The gods, old as night, don't trouble us.
Poor weeping Venus! Her pubic hairs are grey,
and her magic love girdle has lost its spring.
Neptune wonders where he put his trident.
Mars is gaga – illusory vultures on the wing.

Pluto exhumed, blinks. My kind of world, he thinks.
Kidnapping and rape, like my Front Page exploits
adroitly brutal – but he looks out of sorts when
other unmanned gods shake their heads tut tut,
respond boastingly, boringly anecdotal.

Diana has done a bunk, fearing astronauts.
Saturn, Time on his hands, stares at nothing and
nothing stares back. Glum Bacchus talks *ad nauseam*
of cirrhosis and small bald Cupid, fiddling
with arrows, can't recall which side the heart is.

All the old gods have become enfeebled,
mere playthings for poets. Few, doze or daft,
frolic on Parnassian clover. True, sometimes
summer light dies in a room – but only
a bearded profile in a cloud floats over.

In Highgate Woods

Entering the shuffling hush of tamed
Highgate Woods I recall the insolence
of a Polish poet's search for his own coffin.
He wandered through a vast owl–dark forest,
percussed the bark of 200 trees (he wrote)
and, at last, heard the desired woodnote.
He must have been an explorer of a sort,
death–magnetised as are all explorers.

Fantasy can haunt and bedlam itself
into fact; but I'm too old to copy
that poet's half-serious libretto act.
I observe the choreograph of leaf-fall
and dare not tap upon one lordly tree.
Old poets stay at home to become explorers;
the older they get, the smaller they get
and, relentlessly, the trees grow tall.

Portrait of an Old Doctor

Lover of music more than his textbooks'
arrhythmic prose and dated, almost dangerous
his Conybeare and his Boyd's *Pathology*.
(Notes in the margin by the student he was.)

What was it all about? Blunderbuss drugs
prescribed to ease the patient. And moonbeams.
A composer – a Beethoven, a Smetana –
it seemed, could be deaf but not a doctor.

He had been a confidence man for the patient.
That's how it was in The Theatre of Disease
and, at the final act, he had lifted
his stethoscope to listen as if to Mozart.

Then, silently, relatives and friends filed out.
No applause. None for Hippocrates' art.

Winged Back

Strange the potency of a cheap dance tune
Noël Coward

One such winged me back to a different post-code,
to an England that like a translation
almost was, to my muscular days
that were marvellous being ordinary.
365 days, marvellous;

to an England where sweet-rationing ended,
where nature tamely resumed its capture
behind park railings. Few thorns. Fewer thistles;
to *Vivat Regina* and the linseed willow-sound
of Compton and Edrich winning the Ashes.

Elsewhere, Troy always burning. Newspaper stuff.
The recurring decimal of calamity.
Famine. Murder. Pollinating fires.
When they stubbed one out another one flared.
Statesmen lit their cigars from the embers.

They still do. With every enrichment
an injury. They bicker and banquet,

confer and dally, pull on cigars that glow
with blood-light. And all my years,
like the arson of Troy, are elsewhere. Ashes.

Cricket Bat

Reclinate and welded to two gloved hands,
its nervous patting and petting of the crease,
the willow of it, the linseed smell of it,
the long rubbered handle ready for
the shuddering and thrill of a three-spring
slyly leaning winking flagrant leg-glide;

or its skill and pleasure in a kissing shot
through the diving slips, so delicate
so sensual; or its prompt dispatch
of a blatant full-toss. But patience
and the seductive waiting game is all.
So it lusts for the loose one and stonewalls

till, boy, it's up for it, the sex of six,
no longer 45 degrees, but embeamed,
astonishing itself with a head-on sweet
collision – the ball's hung flying silence –
while still upraised, vertical, it salutes
the saluting home pavilion and falls.

Moonbright

Afterwards, late, walking home from hospital,
that December hour too blatantly moonbright
– such an unworldly moon so widely round,
an orifice of scintillating arctic light –
I thought how the effrontery of a similar moon,
a Pirandello moon that could make men howl,
would, in future, bring back the *eidolon*
of you, father, propped high on pillow,
your mouth ajar, your nerveless hand in mine.

At home, feeling hollow, I shamelessly wept
– whether for you or myself I do not know.
Tonight a bracing wind makes my eyes cry
while a cloud dociles an impudent moon
that is and was, and is again, and was.

Men become mortal the night their fathers die.

Sunbright

Sunbright sunbright, you said,
the first time we met in Venice
you, so alive with human light
I was dazzled black;
– like heavy morning curtains
in a sleeping bedroom
suddenly pulled back.

And the first time you undressed,
once more, I, frail-eyed,
undeservedly blessed,
as if it were a holy day,
as if it were yuletide,
and feeling a little drunk,
simply had to look away.

Well, circumspect Henry James
couldn't write *The Turn of the Screw*
till he turned his back on sunbright.
Chair around, just so,
to what was alive, beguiling,
in the Canaletto scene below.

Sweet, all this is true or virtually true.
It's only a poetry-licensed lie
when I rhyme and cheat and wink
and swear I almost need to wear
(muses help me, cross my heart) sunglasses
each time I think of you.

THE SUMMER FRUSTRATIONS
OF DAFYDD AP GWILYM

(Every day I fall in love I do with one or two)

1. Dafydd and the Brecon Deacon's Wife (Storm)

All that July-long languorous Saturday
I, the swarthy one, fawned for her kisses.
Holiday girls are easy and persuasive I was.
I even praised her husband (as I stroked her bum).
'So big in Brecon. So *very* big in Brecon.'

With that Eminent at home, no adder in sight,
at last, in the dark Ceredigion wood we lay.
Then whoops! Zips of sabbath-scolding light
bullied the heights above Cardigan Bay.
Heaven's furniture shifted. My pretty trembled,
leant on one elbow, eyes improbably white.
Up she rose, no arrow swifter, away, away.

Gentlemen, my feelings I'm sure you understand.
Like trying to open a heavy jammed door
and the damned knob comes away in your hand.

Who alerted the gods to have such fun?
(I curse their fervent stupendous din.)
I suppose you could call it, *Celestial Interruptus*,
with me stiff-o, trousers down, saved from sin.

Too bloody powerful her Brecon husband, mun.

2. Dafydd at Llanbadarn

I don't give a monkey-nut for their prissy talk.
Sunday – forgive me, Lord – is an amiable time
to chase the chaste. After church of course.
But no unburdened smile or sweet kiss ever
from one starched lady of Llanbadarn.
And me, so horny, I can hardly walk.

Give them boils, Lord, since none my needs assuage
– not even she whose nose seems like a chair
for spectacles! I ache. If only one, in luck,
roused me in the heather then Garwy himself
would stagger back envious and awestruck.
Lesbians they must be. Give them pox, Lord, and
    age.

When, parasolled, they left the church slow-paced
along the gravel pathway, past the grand
shadow of the yew, I winked, I whispered.

Nun-faced they frowned their strait-laced Never!
So I, as true a stud as Garwy, stand
near graves, full of sperm. Oh what a waste!

3. Dafydd's Night at an English Inn

The wrong side of the border, at the New Inn
beside river reflections of swans and mallards,
the tidy English gave me wary looks.
One did not. Shapely she was and wanton-eyed,
pretty as Morfudd. Of course I played my cards
as waggishly we enjoyed a flask or two.

At dinner, over candle-light, I dared to ask
with Welsh finesse if she would fork my fish
and eat my meat. Nice? The rest of my menu
I won't recite! She half-smiled. Was that a Yes?
In her tight dress her evident bosom heaved.
Too often the dainty ladies I misconstrue
yet twice a day a clock that's stopped is right.

Later, tavern-dark, moon asleep, I sought
her door. Cold my feet on stone. Outstretched my
  hand,

a blind man's. I stumbled, crashed, and copper
  pans
went clamouring on the floor. Bloody dogs began
to bark. (Goodbye one night stand) Out came the
  English,
East and West, lantern–lit, and half undressed:
voyeurs, snobs, poseurs, shouting Robbers! Robbers!

Unmanned, what could I do but join them?
I screamed Robbers! Robbers! louder than the
  rest.

4. Dafydd's Oath

Between gloom-burdened sentinel yews
Morfudd has gone to inhabit the habit of a nun,
bolted and locked in Heaven's Waiting Room.

Big laughter in the Inn. Small laughter in the pews.
With jokes and clerihews I'm peevishly mocked
for in the Alun Valley it's headline news.

Others there were and in dandelion weather I
    worded them.
Few would yield. And the morning after, always,
through the window, I'd see the scarecrow in the
    field.

Priest, in time, write only Morfudd in my dust.
Now she's starched in nun's gown and I, Ovid's man,
am hired to play the clown for Dyddgu's father.

Still, come what may, my ring on heart, I swear
till North star and South star coalesce
I'll be true to Morfudd . . . Well, more or less.

5. Letter Not Sent

Rain again and the jaundiced dandelions
startling the overgrown grass. I miss you, Morfudd,
you with the licit girls of Mary, foreheads hidden,
your husband-hunchback, hell-bent, shouting in
    his glass house,
and I, staring long at these dragon-tongued logs.

For it's so long since our love's tumult, thumbs up,
rhyme-happy, when every delinquent night
I nightingaled you. What was my word-hoard for
if not for your delight? Merely to look at you
I'd ignite into a fine-glowing ember.
Was it all like a promise made in wine?

Once we made a mansion in the greenwood
but summer's over, dulcet one. I'm moon-shot,
love-lorn, lust-locked, thumbs down, imagining

you listening to God's silent silence
— only the rustle of a nun's gown.

But hear me, love. Without you I'm in motley cloth
without a cause — just a funny bard who plays the
  clown
for princely money, not for your favours and
  applause.

The bully clock strikes the hour. The tall yews wait
  for all.
Now say that I'm yours as scarecrows are lonely;
else goodnight and I will sing and pluck
harp's most secret and deepest string for Dyddgu.

Last Visit of Uncle Isidore

No more magic tricks from Uncle Isidore.
The rain–dishevelled roses in their extremity
could have guessed the party was over.
Indoors, long past tea–time, Great Uncle Isidore,
distant relative not always distant,
stayed and stayed. So did the visiting rain.

Mama always said, 'Poor Isidore.' And he was poor.
Wearing my father's old clothes Uncle creaked
    'Ouch'
and cursed Arthritis.
                'Not fair. People should suffer
their illnesses when they're young and healthy.'

My elder brother slammed the front door goodbye.
The raincoat-smelling bus would take him
to Tonypandy where the miners assembled
to jeer Oswald Mosley and the police.
                'Uncle Isidore, work?'
my brother had said, 'For decades he did nothing
and he didn't even do that till after lunch.'

For one year Uncle played a violin
for the silent pictures at the Coronet Cinema.

Then he retired.
            'At the same age as Jesus
when he was crucified,' he half-boasted.

Mama left for the kettle in the kitchen.
Uncle, in the armchair, muttered 'I don't feel well.'
He seemed to fall asleep with his eyes open,
staring at nothing, and his face became
a forgery of itself. Was this one of his tricks?

I wanted to go out, play with Philip Griffiths.
At the window I whispered,
                        'Rain, rain go to Spain,
                        Come again another day.'

Bluebells

Cycling for the bluebells near St Mellons
two boys tasted the decomposing of the light
in a high echoing tunnel. They stopped,
left foot on the pedal, right foot on the ground,
to lark loudly, My hen Glad is sad aye!

When Keith shouted I DON'T BELIEVE IN GOD
believe in God.. in God.. in God a sudden
   WHOOSH replied. Four pupils dilated.
Tachycardia. A goods train clumped over
and multitudinous thunderbolts shrivelled.

Later, bikes angled against a stout tree,
they heard a meandering bee shopping among the
   profusion of flowers they bent
to pick. Keith said, Devout little bugger.
Sounds like a daft insect's prayer to me.

Through the returning dark tunnel they hurled
echoes and laughed. But the small dot remained
below the big question mark when they came out
(bluebells alive in the handlebar baskets)
blessed in the unanswering light of the world.

Scent

Lately, going in and out of the house
we once shared, I sometimes think
that the dead have many disguises;
so I hesitate at the blue-painted gatepost
– there where the evening midges dance –
because of the propinquity of a twining shrub
you long ago planted – now in jubilating flower
and surrendering faintly
its button-holding scent – one so alluring,
so delinquent, it could have made Adam
fall on Eve, with delight, in Eden.

In this world the scent could have haunted
the sacred gardens of Athens
to distract a philosopher from his thoughts,
or wafted through an open window
of the Great Library in Alexandria
unbidden, prompting a scholar
to uplift his eyes from his scroll.

But what do I care about that.
For me, now, you are its sole tenant.
Compelled I linger, allowing myself

the charm and freedom of inebriating fancy
till the scent becomes only the scent itself
returning, and I, at the gate, like Orpheus,
sober, alone, and a little wretched.

2012

The Bus

Llantwit Major to Bridgend

At the gnat-employed sundown, all shadows long,
the last bus of the summer day bestirred,
then laboured away from Llantwit Major
without one passenger towards the sheepfields.

At each approaching bus stop on the coast road
no-one waited, not even at Marcross's presbyterian-
   grey
Post Office shop. Undeterred, the bus, zestful,
passed low dry-stone walls, high hedges, stonecrop.

After St Bride's, a postcard view: to the West
the unrestful sway of the sea, its water-light
stretching beyond the wreck-loving Tusker Rock
to a soul-feast of horizon colour.

But no expectant traveller at Ogmore
hailed the driver – only a fuss of sheep
on the crepuscular road. There, the bus idled
before blustering on to Bridgend's bus station.

Bridgend to Llantwit Major

After a mug of sweet tea and a fag
the driver backed the bus out of its dolorous
berth, steered it into the incurious
busy mainstreet and lamplit dusk of the town.

Three brisk miles, then another three miles.
Still not one man, not one woman boarded
the bus. The sea had begun its night shift,
the great night was spawning its stars.

The driver, proud of his bus, felt depressed.
Nobody. Why? It was demeaning. Back and fore,
what was the point of it all unless
the journey exploded into meaning?

He drove inland with serious celerity
passed familiar oncoming hedges.
On schedule, at the terminus of Llantwit,
the bus arrived empty, yet terrific with light.

Parrotscold

This night in your ordinary unhappiness
dine alone at L'artista not because of the fussy
authoritarian Emperor of Habit. You're timid,
you know the tiredness of doing nothing,

and your old age is chilled with prudence.
Are there also amyloid moths in your memory?
It's your anniversary, stupid. Isn't her name writ
more in your blood than on bloodless stone?

You say, Every day is our anniversary Maybe,
but tonight forget to finger-fumble your small
world's wounds. Praise instead your dead ally,
your tactful guide, your Beatrice unsurpassed

who for sweet pampered decades shared your bed
and board. (Think! Dante only saw his Beatrice
twice). Now, mast broken, lone helmless years pass
and stone too may crumble. Nothing lasts except

nothing; yet though Beatrice is no more and
    nothing,
Beatrice is, her shadow hidden in the shade.
So this nightfall, with all your debts to her
unpaid, raise high and higher the full red glass.

A Story

Dear one, tell me a story of elsewhere,
a story young from times of old
when the bees of Hybla were hushed
in the perfumed air – and did not sting.

Tell me a story of honeyed intent,
of a door that was opened slowly for
the improbable Angel of Happiness
but only a beggar was there

and the olive leaves behind him shaken
for nothing in the world was still
till the door was closed, the wine-glass filled,
and the empty chair at the table taken.

Parable

Now summer has come to my garden
and a thing of phenogamous beauty
   has come
half hidden below the shadow darkness
   of a bush.
Almost luminous, it peeps from behind a leaf
with a daring redness that commands Stop!
Admire me.

Not a proud Lawrentian geranium,
not an opium-tranced poppy or luscious rose
of improvident scent.
What?
To know its name I buy a colour-plated
encyclopaedia of flowers.
Not listed there.

This morning I open the front door
to two sombre strangers.
They carry night-black, official-looking books
and religious tracts.
Do you know the end of the world is nigh?

I reply Yes and they are manifestly disappointed.
When I confess I keep a packed suitcase
ready upstairs,
they retreat with Olympic pace.

Afterwards, I happen to glance at my nameless
little red flower.
It seems even more beautiful than before.

Vows

1. A Galway Story

After the humility of prayer,
in a room sauced with holiness,
the dying man of Galway lay in his past
and his friend hoarsely swore
to sustain his wife with roses and violets
and very fine parsley.

But soon this friend, without a nod or a no,
vanished like a flame blown out (where?)
only to return twenty-nine years later,
diamond-studded, ravished and grey,
to offer the once-fair widow roses and violets
and very fine parsley.

Displeased, bristling, she began to undress. Slow.
Slow. Dropped her silks. Then he heard her say,
'You're released from your vow for here are my
    roses
my violets and my very fine parsley.' Insolently
the friend of her husband swiftly turned away,
vanished without a nod or a no.

2. Hiraeth

More drawl of American South than Welsh lilt
yet proud of his lineage. (He liked his beer strong!)
'One day I'll take my kitbag home,' he vowed.
'Rugby's my religion, the Dragon's my flag.'

He was a pensioner when BA flew him back
in '88. 'Wales is still great,' he'd brag, 'despite
Thatcher. It's a thrill to be home, to belong.'
I met him at the Match. He wore a daffodil.

For decades he'd fed cuttings to his scrapbook:
From Dylan's wild funeral to the miners' strike;
Welsh things. 'I'd like to be buried here,' he said
quietly. I felt a chill and made a joke.

That lightless day they scampered for a try, failed –
and still defeated voices wailed 'Gwlad, Gwlad,'
while spiteful silks of rain sulkingly fell
on neighbouring macs that smelt of stale.

3. The Cuneiform Tablet

When the land became a hill
and a dark canyon,
capsizing the village homes,
did he not take my sister
like a wolf in the sheepfold
leaving her with child?
As the Storm-god sought revenge
so shall I.

To the Mighty Mother-womb
I spit this vow.
I'll put a yoke on him
till his joints bend not
and his large eyes collapse.
He shall become more meat than man
in a pool of blood, in a pyre of fire.
Never will his smoke-spirit know rest
in the nether world.
Vermin will devour him
and the worm fall from his nose.

I shall appropriate
his jaspers and his ivories
his goats and his guinea-fowl,
slaughter his six sons,
but spare his elder women-folk.
As for my disgraced sister
I shall slit her throat cleanly
rather than she be stoned.
Storm-god, would you be
as merciful?
Mighty Mother-womb
Am I not justified?

4. Peace in our Time

When they vow
a subtle perfume,
tactful dilutions
of musk, civet, ambergris,

expect a computer error:
a veritable gasworks.
Dry in the vibrating air
plain H_2S.

When they promise
a hundredpiece orchestra,
Brahms, Berlioz, Mahler −
Three Blind Mice on a comb.

When a King's golden crown,
a party paper hat;
when a Queen's diamond,
a globule of glass.

When a champagne night
at the Ritz
with stunning Delilah,
a haircut.

When a faultless racehorse

like Desert Orchid
or Red Rum,
a donkey.

When 100 virgins in heaven
none quite as old
as Methuselah . . .
Pardon?

Consider the double suicide pact
of Mr and Mrs Malby.
As agreed, he shot her first,
then was unable.

Gently he undressed her,
as he had in life:
he propped her up
naked in the bath.

Night after night
brought lit candles
into that bathroom
where he quietly dined;

faithfully choosing
her favourite dishes –
fish mainly, turbot, trout,
kindly removing the bones.

In Black Ink

(Anniversary poem for Leo)

Seen through a tear the world's a blur.
No rainbow on an eyelash.

It was the morning of the black tie
– no confident peacock strut.
Mourners under dark umbrellas.

Yit-ga-dal ve-yit-ka-dash . . .

In the house behind shut gates
the sadness of unused things.
All was grievous-grey, all was plain
as the stony tablets of the law;
and I thought how I used to scold you
for your peacock's display on Budget Day,
how then, mischievous, you'd scald me,
'You're so bourgeois, so tame. Be bold,
pitch your tent beneath Vesuvius.'

Once together by Roath Park Lake,
at the slow-motion sunset hour,
we both were blessed and dressed in colour.

Dear brother, M.P. for Happiness, master-
politician, what an elative time
to recite the gospel of the secular!

Later, to those dispossessed, defeated,
in doldrums or in perdition,
you'd render all the light you were.

Now you've been dead three war-scoured years
and your Joseph coat's in rags. The sun's
retreated. Winter weather. And I recall
the sour chant of Hebrew prayer.

Yit-ga-dal ve-yit-ka-dash . . .

'Stubborn', you said. 'I had to be stubborn
to pass each Bill.' Back home ex-miners
sang in hunger, 'Bread of Heaven'.

Outrageous One, I write these lines for you
in modest ink, with fraternal love,
and hear the mocking laughter of the dead.
You wink, you sigh, 'Use a peacock's feather.'

The Girl in the Kitchen

(Evan Walters, 1938)

1

The key's been turned, the kitchen door's ajar.
In the secrecy of silence she who calls me 'sir'
does not know I'm here, watching her,
a licensed voyeur, watching her –
only a shout away and yet so far.

She vexes me. She's unsure, rough, and humble,
but dare I clear my throat, discreetly cough,
enter the bright instant? Or close the door
quietly, turn the key? I have seen enough.
On the canvas I shall possess her double.

2

I do 'oover, I do dust, I do make
the coal-grate glow. When I'm on my knees to scrub
sir stares at my be'ind as if it were
a firebomb. I know them artists. Each one's
a bloody peeping Tom. I don't mind.

I look into a soap-bubble and see us wed;
me with a fag, sir with a cigar. I'd still

prepare 'is food, stitchin' to mend, but I'd drive
'is car. 'E'd paint me nude. I'd be a star –
'is pitcher called, 'Beauty in the kitchen'.

Both Eyes Open

When one shuts one eye one does not hear everything
Swiss Proverb

The tall painter has painted the small painter
in front of his easel. With one eye shut he sees
a landscape after refreshments of rain.
Pearls on grass blades. Nature's jewelry shop.

Look closer. Beneath a mirror of a tree
a girl just visible in a dark skirt.
It must be that both painters love reticence
else her skirt would be a fiery yellow.

In this world that's a mirror of the world
the tall painter paints for the small painter
a bird in the tree that cannot be seen
and a girl in a skirt he'd rather not see.

I'm coming to think that this painted world
is a familiar — one visited within a mirror
or more likely dreamed about, both eyes open,
where I walked through gateways to that other world.

Listen! the girl in a fiery yellow skirt

is entranced by the singing bird hidden in the tree
which neither of the painters painted.
I wait for it to fly out of the frame.

Blue Song

Some things there always are,
some things a man must lose.
Picasso paints a guitar,
that way he sings the Blues.

Russian cows jump over the moon
(very strong is Russian booze)
but Chagall's cow never lands,
otherwise he'd sing the Blues.

O'Keefe paints flowers in close-up
and critics look for Freudian clues.
Female genitalia. Voyeur!
No wonder the lady sings the Blues.

Is that a telephone or a lobster?
Surely Salvador is confused.
He says, Dial the phone and hear
the lobster trying to sing the Blues.

Rothko squares a mirror with blood
(there's blood in his every bruise),
paints his own reflection out
and soundlessly sings the Blues.

Pale moon-faced Francis Bacon
eerily shrieks and spews
humanoid freaks into a cage.
Odd way to sing the Blues.

Body-detective Lucian Freud
magnifies his sexless nudes
– the uglier the better.
That's how he sings the Blues.

The aloneness of the artist!
So Hockney paints his trees in twos
and Time, itself, in colours passing.
A covert way to sing the Blues.

Damian likes his sheep well-pickled,
I prefer my meat in stews.
Let collectors shed their millions.
Soon they'll sing the Blues.

Is Tracy Emin's messy bed
pertinent British art? J'accuse.
Not for sexpence would I sleep in it
to stop her bawling out her Blues.

Do I wish to be a painter
acclaimed with buffs' reviews?
All I lack is talent,
that's why I sing the Blues.

Perspectives

(5 paragraphs for Frank O'Hara)

I sit in L'artista, our local Italian restaurant.
Outside, a rain-thrashed queue waits for their bus.
At an adjacent table, a man with liquorice hair
is shouting to himself; but soon I discover
he's phoning someone. At 1.50 p.m. I order
Fusilli all' Ortolana and their house-red poison.

A waitress bending forward to pick up a spoon
bothers me in more ways than two.
She moves with such grace and femininity
the very earth is richer where she stands.
It surely makes all the clientele forget
their 'nostalgia for the infinite' and to understand,
perhaps for the first time, 'the nostalgia of the
    infinite'.

Umbrellas pass by the window as I eat my pasta.
Some of it spills onto my trousers, dammit.
Why does this make me think how those poets
who write enigmatic nonsense become famously
the darlings of the professors they most despise?

At 2.23 p.m. I drink my cappuccino and glance
at the TV that's flitting behind the counter.
The 2012 dogs of war are pissing on the dead,
  Frank.
It could be Syria. Could be Afghanistan.

At 2.40 p.m. the Renoir beautiful one
brings me the bill (£15.10p). She squawks. Pity
her voice like a very active yak makes me shiver.
Outside the rain's gone North. A 2.41 droplet
of pure silver falls from a high tin roof.

Pre-Xmas at L'artista

Sorcery of music! Listening to it some, as in sleep,
become inexact imitations of themselves.
Others, also out of Time, return into another.

When the ugliest beggar you ever saw,
an old soldier's ribbon across his chest,
limped into L'artista, evidently knackered,
to sing Silent Night with such uncanny rapture
the woman at the corner-table, beneath the
    balloons,
baring her left breast for her baby
began to resemble the brooding figure
in Giorgione's *Tempesta*; our seductive
waitress became a shy Botticelli angel;
L'artista's elegant boss framed in the doorway
posed like the Grand Doge in Gritti's portrait;
and at the long scheming table
a Xmas staff party, no longer rowdy,
seemed ready to model for *The Last Supper*.

The crippled beggar collected his silver
and I thought how beautiful an ugly man can be.
When he opened the door to the outside world
no cool draught was felt from a great beating wing.

Simply, the resident TV resumed its appalling dominance with scenes of the most debauched, most up-to-date massacre of the innocents with haggard Rachel weeping for her children.

A Fan

Too many flaws: my poem less fresh than tinned
but he was one who would never let me fail.
His first sedative gust of praise turned
into an imperious fountain, would not pause,
he pointing out nuances I didn't intend
and I smiled Cheese until I became stale
and I thought of luminous William Blake
enthusing, '*That* is sheer genius,'
and Constable replying, 'Gosh, and there's me
thinking it was only a painting.'

Vignette: High Street after Rain

Sun, suddenly, leaps through, hoopla!
and outside the jewelry shop,
in bravado opposition,
riots of electric raindrops,
hanging from a wire, switch on.

A settled rain pool on the pavement
in slow slow-motion seems to drink
itself up, shrinks, already forgets
the joyous ejaculations of the storm,
will leave behind only its shadow.

Near the pharmacy, the two washed trees
in their best new green, so feminine,
whose gossipy branches interlock, nod
to discuss their rain-pricked leaf-shock
and the Pathetic Fallacy!

Now ladder-high above the rooftops
tantrums of seagulls appear
so soon to disappear,
their wings becoming ever more tiny
like handkerchiefs waving goodbye.

Wasp

At 3 p.m. I'm sitting in L'artista
as usual, bored, waiting for something unusual.
London's under the weather, has become prose.
Don't tell me I should be in the country
watching hypnotised animals standing
motionless in the gloom of an afternoon.

Here, at least, I'm entertained by a wasp:
it hovers near the windowsill's waxen flowers;
deluded, it dives for nectar. Afterwards in anger,
the wasp that does not know it's a wasp
becomes a little, loud, nazi insect-official.
Oblivious, in come two Jewish beards.

Next to my table they seem to discuss Theology
— much concern about the state of a soul —
but soon, like the wasp, I twig I'm deceived
when one takes his boot off to prove his point.
Then the other remarks, 'Well, the heel's all right.'

Look! They're being served by the over-powdered,
rose-beautiful, yakking waitress. Now the wasp
decides to bully them. Who reckons a rose
is a rose is a rose? Not always, it ain't.

As for me, when I talk to myself,
I do not know whom I'm addressing.

The wasp flies to the windowpane, to its prison.
So human! The door opens to the greater noise
of traffic. Enter two youthful lovers,
enter the world. Inexhaustible
the possibilities of what happens next.

Cats

One Saturday afternoon in Istanbul
on waste ground fit for a parking lot
not far from the Galata Bridge,
the hullabaloo of two cats copulating.

We observed a man built like a poster-hero,
one savage arm raised, a stone in his fist.

Cats in England are private creatures.
They fuck in private as Englishmen do.

Different country. Different cats.

Yet they make an inhuman noise
just as the English do.

I uttered an unarmoured, 'Leave 'em alone.'
The poster-hero ignored me
as much as the busy cats ignored him.
He stooped, he weighed another stone.

On behalf of the British Council (who had hired me)
and all animal lovers
(these two cats were animal lovers!)

not to mention D.H. Lawrence
and the sanctity of love-making
(the subject of my future lecture)
I asked my translator to translate.

After a protein-rich Turkish dialogue
the muscular No of a man
continued to shower stones on the cats
and the cats continued their joyous coupling.

'He's stoning them,' explained my translator,
'because he says they're both male cats.'

Grimly I stared at the grim poster-hero and
the more I stared the more he grew
more muscular. I turned away without valour
and soon, as if by appointment,
we encountered an unjudging beggar.
Gratefully, I dropped a few coins in his cap.

Song of the Crow

'From faraway, I,
messenger of malign news,
flew under reversing clouds
fast as my shadow
on the waters below.
Never resting. Another 100 miles,
then again another 100 miles,
me and my little black shadow,
simply to find your town,
your street, your home,
your face at the window.'

So it sang its gride song
and I heard it
beyond the glass,
shabby, hopping on the snow,
this way, that way,
to fall silent at last,
to look about furtively,
that way, *this* way,

before marking with vicious beak
a cross in the snow.

Then it stretched its black wings wide.

(*After Primo Levi*)

Wagner

After the sick adventure and insolence
of steep soaring notes, heaven-lit,
the romantic convulsive fall and
fall to nuances of German black.

The suited orchestra inhabit the pit –
like the dead must be hidden.
Cthonic music must come back as if
bidden from the deeps of the earth.

Wagner, is this your dream or Wotan's?
An organ dismembered, a sexual shout,
scream and burn – climax of a candle-flame
blown out, more a woman's than a man's.

Genius with the soul of a vulture
your overgrown music is good for heroes,
for cheap Hollywood; yet there's something else,
something taciturn, almost remembered.

Outside the Hall even your statue, moon-blown,
stone-deaf, smells of the urn; and ghosts soaped
in moonlight weep. The streets of Germany
are clean, like the hands of Lady Macbeth.

And does your stern distinguished statue keep
vigil for another Fuhrer's return?
Some statues never awaken,
some never seem to sleep.

Rilke's Confession

Whoever weeps somewhere in the night
without comfort
mimics me

Whoever laughs somewhere in the night
without cause
frightens me

Whoever wanders somewhere in the night
without purpose
counsels me

Whoever screams somewhere in the night
without mercy
bruises me

Whoever makes love somewhere in the night
without love
rebukes me

Whoever dies somewhere in the night
with no-one by
precedes me

Side Effects

Ghosts released from Time walked into the world
    of light −
a drug's mistake, this glimpse of the other world.
I was close to Eternity the other night.

I observed the evolution of angels into birds
and Lilith screaming, her umbilical cord tied to
    earth.
I won't repeat the demonic squalor of her words.

The shock of the Old! Permanent her fate, her
    frailty.
Her scream changed into an ambulance's siren
when they hurried me back in time to Casualty.

Now home from Zohar's frantic country where
    Death dies
I celebrate the Big Bang, strange thing born of a
    mistake,
beautiful side-effect, magic of sundown and sunrise,

this Earth unbalanced and spinning among the
    stars.

Gone?

Always I wanted to hear the heartbeat
of words and summoned you, oneiric one.
I changed your feathers to purple and to white.

So what did you, ventriloquist bird, say
besides, It's closing time, old dear?
You only spoke when compelled –

as when the long whistle blew on happiness
or when sunlight was such a dazzle
you flew into it, thinking you could sing.

Wide awake or half asleep you liked to be
deceptive, yet never babblative enough
to employ the bald serious scholars.

Odd that you imagined you could wear
and blend purple feathers with the white
to abate the panic of a blank page.

When I fed you with my two lives you took
your fill of both and soliloquised.
Always your style was in the error.

Sometimes you choired loudly, dionysiac
(the drama of an exclamation mark!)
and sometimes you word-whispered sedately.

Now I'm tired and you nest elsewhere.
Bird, your cage is empty. Will you come back?
I see no feathers in the wind.